Gazpacho Cookbook

Discover the Delicious Delights of Cold Soups with these Amazing Gazpacho Recipes

By
BookSumo Press

Published by
http://www.booksumo.com

LEGAL NOTES

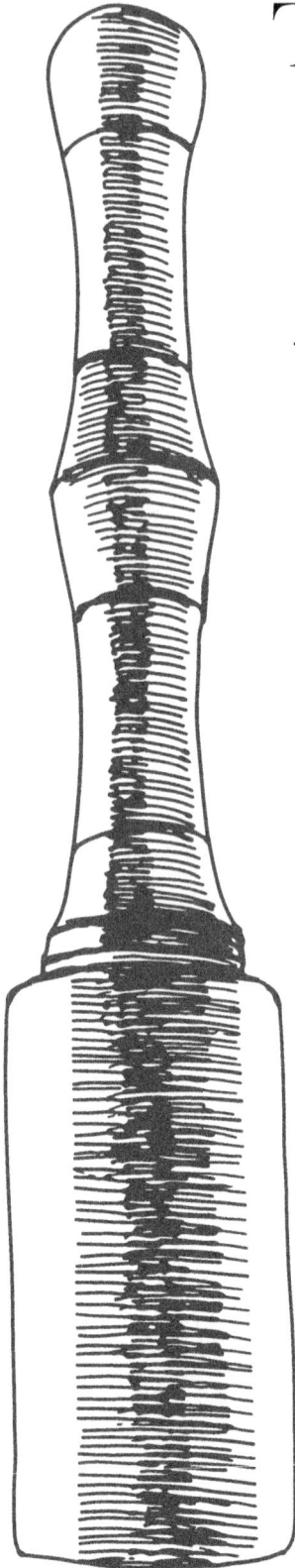

Table of Contents

West Coast
Gazpacho

Prep Time: 15 mins
Total Time: 15 mins

Servings per Recipe: 4
Calories   389.3
Fat   36.7g
Cholesterol   0.0mg
Sodium   29.4mg
Carbohydrates   16.0g
Protein   3.3g

Ingredients

2 C. yellow pear tomatoes, sliced in half
2 yellow bell peppers, seeds removed and diced
1 red bell pepper, seeds removed and diced
1 cucumber, peeled, seeds removed and diced
1 bunch green onion, chopped
3 cloves garlic, diced
1 bunch cilantro, destemmed and finely chopped

1 jalapeno, seeds removed and diced
2/3 C. olive oil
3 tbsps white wine vinegar
3 tbsps finely chopped fresh chives
salt, to taste
fresh coarse ground black pepper, to taste

Directions

1. Get a bowl, mix: jalapeno, tomatoes, cilantro, pepper, garlic, onions, and cucumbers.
2. Get a 2nd bowl, combine: herbs, olive oil, and white vinegar.
3. Stir the mix then add in some pepper and salt.
4. Combine both bowls and let the gazpacho for 1 hr, covered in the fridge.
5. Enjoy.

ROMAN
Gazpacho

Prep Time: 25 mins
Total Time: 25 mins

Servings per Recipe: 6

Calories	63.8
Fat	0.4g
Cholesterol	0.0mg
Sodium	368.6mg
Carbohydrates	13.9g
Protein	2.3g

Ingredients

1 1/2 lbs ripe tomatoes, seeded, cut into
2 inch pieces
1 large cucumber, peeled, halved
lengthwise, seeded, and sliced into 1/2
inch slices
1 red bell pepper, cut into 1 inch pieces
1 small red onion, coarsely chopped
2 cloves garlic, diced
1 1/2 C. tomato juice

1/3 C. balsamic vinegar
1/2 tsp salt
1/4 tsp red pepper flakes
1/3 C. chopped fresh basil, for garnish

Directions

1. Add the following to the bowl of a food processor: garlic, tomatoes, onion, bell peppers, and cucumbers.
2. Chop the veggies then combine in the pepper flakes, tomato juice, salt, and vinegar.
3. Continue to combine the mix a few more times.
4. Then pour everything into a bowl and place a covering of plastic on the bowl.
5. Put everything in the fridge for 8 hrs.
6. Add in some more pepper and salt and divide the mix between serving bowls.
7. Top each serving with some basil.
8. Enjoy.

Sourdough
Gazpacho

Prep Time: 15 mins
Total Time: 15 mins

Servings per Recipe: 6
Calories   135.1
Fat   5.4g
Cholesterol   0.0mg
Sodium   469.3mg
Carbohydrates   20.5g
Protein   3.8g

Ingredients

2 tbsps extra virgin olive oil
3 large garlic cloves, diced
6 large ripe tomatoes, peeled and chopped
1 yellow bell pepper, chopped
1 yellow onion, peeled and chopped
1 large cucumber, peeled and chopped
6 tbsps white wine vinegar
1 slice sourdough bread, crusts removed, soaked in water and squeezed dry
1 tsp salt
1/2 tsp fresh ground pepper

6 drops Tabasco sauce, to taste
1/2 C. grape tomatoes, quartered
1/2 C. yellow bell pepper, chopped
1/2 C. cucumber, peeled and chopped
1/2 C. scallion, chopped

Directions

1. Begin to stir fry your garlic in olive oil for 2 mins then shut the heat.
2. Get a bowl, combine: garlic and oil, tomatoes, bread, yellow pepper, vinegar, cucumbers, and onions.
3. Add the mix to the bowl of a food processor and begin to puree everything.
4. Once the mix is smooth place everything in a bowl and stir in some tabasco, pepper, and salt.
5. Place a covering of plastic on the bowl and put everything in the fridge for 60 mins.
6. Dice the following veggies as the gazpacho chills: grape tomatoes, bell peppers, cucumbers, and scallions.
7. Divide the chopped veggies between the gazpacho when serving everything.
8. Enjoy.

MINTY
Gazpacho

Prep Time: 10 mins
Total Time: 2 hrs 10 mins

Servings per Recipe: 6
Calories	114.7
Fat	7.1g
Cholesterol	0.0mg
Sodium	27.7mg
Carbohydrates	12.2g
Protein	2.2g

Ingredients

2 thick slices onions
1 large beet, roasted and peeled
6 oz. cucumbers, peeled and coarsely chopped
2 lbs ripe tomatoes, quartered
2 sticks celery, coarsely chopped
2 large garlic cloves, halved, green germs removed
2 tbsps sherry wine vinegar, plus a little

extra for the onion
3 tbsps extra virgin olive oil
salt
1/2-1 C. ice water
1/2 C. diced cucumber
slivered fresh mint leaves

Directions

1. Let your onions sit submerged in water then add in a bit of vinegar.
2. Leave the onions to stand for 10 mins.
3. Then slice the onions.
4. Add the following to the bowl of a food processor and puree them: onions, beets, cucumbers, tomatoes, celery, garlic, wine vinegar, olive oil.
5. Puree the mix for 3 mins then place everything into a bowl.
6. Place a covering of plastic on the bowl and put everything in the fridge 3 hrs.
7. Enjoy.

Two Grapes
and Sherry
Gazpacho

Prep Time: 5 mins
Total Time: 25 mins

Servings per Recipe: 4
Calories   1306.0
Fat   122.8g
Cholesterol   10.0mg
Sodium   401.9mg
Carbohydrates   44.2g
Protein   19.6g

Ingredients

3 large garlic cloves
2 C. diced stale bread, crusts removed
2 C. peeled fried and salted almonds
1 C. white seedless grapes, halved
1 C. red seedless grapes, halved
salt
1 1/2 C. extra virgin olive oil
1 1/2-2 tbsps sherry wine vinegar
extra virgin olive oil, as needed
1/4 C. diced bread
salt

1/2 C. mixed red and white seedless grapes,
cut into small dice
1/4 C. peeled fried and salted almonds
1 scallion, thinly sliced diagonally
almond oil or extra virgin olive oil, for
drizzling
sherry wine vinegar, as needed

Directions

1. Get your pieces of garlic boiling in water for 2 mins then remove all the liquids and place the garlic in a bowl, in a the fridge.

2. Place your bread in bowl with water as well and let the bread sit submerged for 12 mins.

3. Now drain the water from the bread and squeeze the bread with your hands to remove more liquids.

4. Place the following in the bowl of a food processor: pieces of garlic, almonds, bread, and grapes.

5. Add some salt and puree the mix.

6. Get 1 C. of cold water and another with olive oil then gradually pour in both liquids into the puree with a slow speed.

7. Now combine in 1.5 tbsps of vinegar and some more salt as well.

8. Place the gazpacho in a bowl and place a covering of plastic on the bowl.

9. Put everything in the fridge for 3 hrs.

10. Now set your oven to 400 degrees before doing anything else.
11. Coat your pieces of bread with olive oil and salt then place everything into a casserole dish.
12. Cook the bread in the oven for 9 mins then place them in a bowl with the scallions, almonds, and grapes.
13. Add in some pepper, salt, some olive oil, and some vinegar.
14. Divide your gazpacho between serving dishes and top each dish with some of the scallion mix. Enjoy.

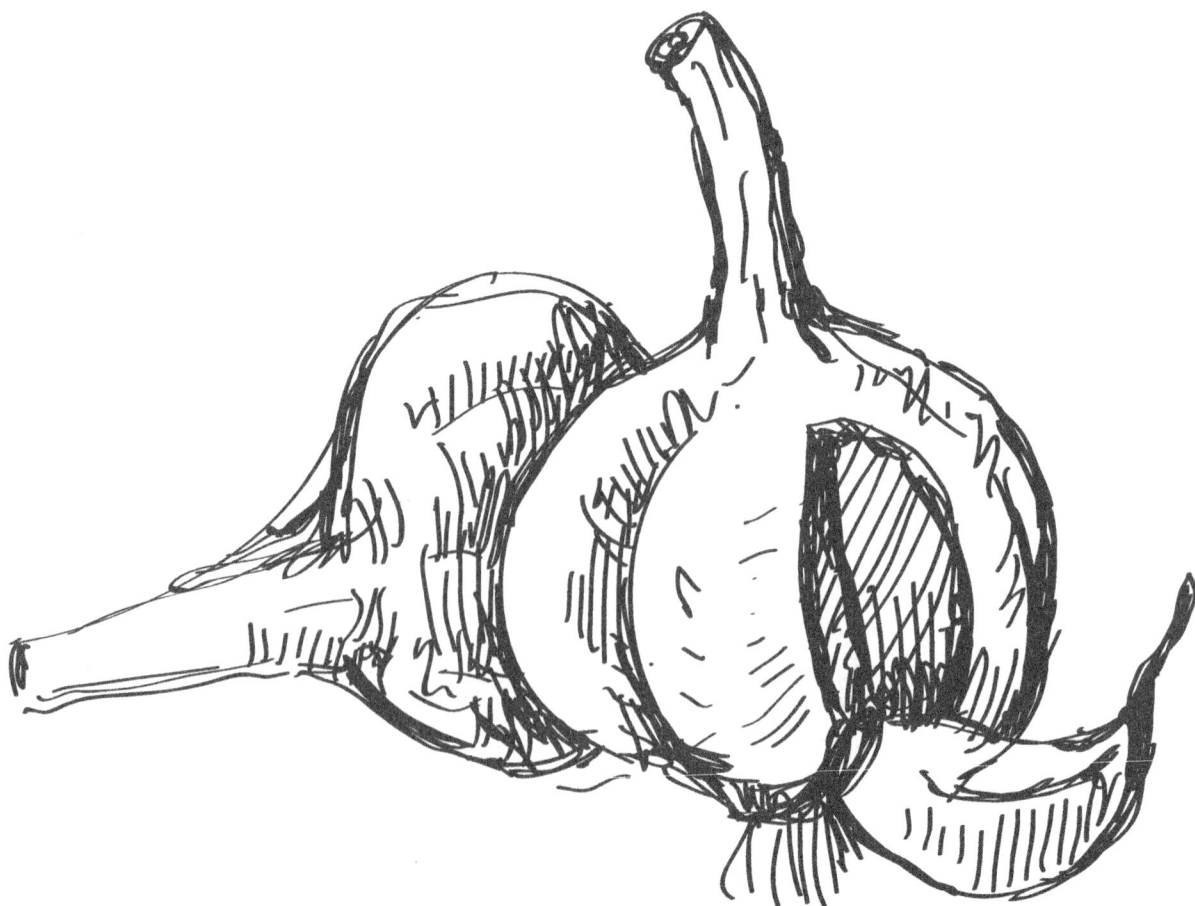

Spaghetti
Gazpacho

Prep Time: 15 mins
Total Time: 35 mins

Servings per Recipe: 6
Calories   155.8
Fat   2.1g
Cholesterol   4.4mg
Sodium   98.0mg
Carbohydrates   27.7g
Protein   7.0g

Ingredients

6 oz. spaghetti, uncooked
vegetable oil cooking spray
1 C. broccoli floret
1 C. carrot, thinly sliced
1 C. zucchini, sliced
1/4 C. onion, sliced
1 small yellow sweet pepper, julienned
1/2 C. cucumber, sliced

1/2 C. fresh mushrooms, sliced
1 small tomatoes, cut into 8 wedges
2 tbsps dry vermouth
6 tbsps grated parmesan cheese
1 tbsp fresh parsley, diced
1/4 tsp sweet red pepper flakes

Directions

1. Get your pasta boiling in water and salt for 9 mins then remove all the liquids.
2. Begin to stir fry your broccoli, carrots, zucchini, and onions, in a frying pan with nonstick spray for 6 mins then combine in the mushrooms, cucumbers, and yellow pepper.
3. Continue to stir fry everything for 6 more mins then combine in the vermouth, tomato, and pasta.
4. Stir the mix and cook everything for 3 mins.
5. Top the pasta mix with the pepper flakes, cheese, and parsley.
6. Enjoy.

INTER
Solstice Gazpacho

Prep Time: 20 mins
Total Time: 1 hr 20 mins

Servings per Recipe: 4
Calories   200.6
Fat   11.3g
Cholesterol   0.0mg
Sodium   636.2mg
Carbohydrates   23.6g
Protein   4.5g

Ingredients

2 1/2 C. water, for blending
1 slice day-old white bread, crusts removed, torn into pieces
2 oz. blanched almonds
2 garlic cloves, fresh, skinned, roughly chopped
1 tbsp olive oil

1 tbsp white wine vinegar
1 tsp salt
2 1/2 C. water, for diluting
1 bunch white grapes, small

Directions

1. Add the following to the bowl of a food processor: water, white bread, almonds, cloves, olive oil, and vinegar.
2. Puree the mx until you have a smooth thick liquid then add a bit more salt and vinegar if you like.
3. Place the mix in a bowl and place a covering of plastic on the bowl.
4. Put everything in the fridge for 60 mins until it is cold then divide the gazpacho between serving dishes.
5. Serve with some grapes.
6. Enjoy.

Gazpacho
Medley

🥣 Prep Time: 15 mins
🕐 Total Time: 15 mins

Servings per Recipe: 6	
Calories	161.8
Fat	12.5g
Cholesterol	0.0mg
Sodium	87.0mg
Carbohydrates	12.3g
Protein	2.4g

Ingredients

2 lbs ripe tomatoes, peeled, seeded, and coarsely chopped
1 medium sweet onion, coarsely chopped
1 large cucumber, peeled and coarsely chopped
1/2 green bell pepper, coarsely chopped
1/2 red bell pepper, coarsely chopped
2 scallions, coarsely chopped
3 garlic cloves
3 tbsps sherry wine vinegar or 3 tbsps balsamic vinegar

1/3 C. extra virgin olive oil
1 - 2 tsp hot pepper sauce
1 tsp ground cumin
1/2-1 C. chilled tomato juice
salt & freshly ground black pepper, to taste
Garnishes
croutons or chopped fresh herbs or sliced scallions or diced avocado

Directions

1. Get a bowl, combine: garlic, tomatoes, scallions, onion, bell peppers, and cucumbers.
2. Place half of the mix into a food processor and puree everything then add in the rest and continue to puree the mix.
3. Place everything back into the bowl and combine in the cumin, olive oil, hot sauce, and vinegar.
4. Stir the mix then add in the tomato juice and continue to stir.
5. Keep an eye on the amount of tomato mix you are adding, try to find a consistency that you enjoy.
6. Add in some black pepper and salt and stir the mix again.
7. Place a covering of plastic on the bowl and place everything in the fridge for 2 hours.
8. Now stir the mix and divide everything between serving bowls and add in some diced avocado, croutons, scallions, and herbs.
9. Enjoy.

GINGER
Gazpacho

Prep Time: 20 mins
Total Time: 20 mins

Servings per Recipe: 4
Calories	104.2
Fat	0.7g
Cholesterol	0.0mg
Sodium	161.1mg
Carbohydrates	25.6g
Protein	3.1g

Ingredients

3 large very ripe tomatoes, cored, seeded, and cut up
2 medium cucumbers, seeded and cut up
2 medium orange sweet bell pepper, seeded and cut up
1 jalapeno, seeded and cut up
1 garlic clove, diced
1/3 C. lime juice

2 tbsps honey
2 tbsps fresh cilantro leaves
1 1/2 tsps grated fresh ginger
1/4 tsp sea salt
ice cube
lime wedges and green onion
v- 8 juice (optional)

Directions

1. Get a bowl, mix: garlic, tomatoes, sweet pepper, and cucumber.
2. Add half of the mix to the bowl of a food processor and puree the mix until it is chunky then add in the rest of the mix and puree everything again.
3. Combine in 1/4 C. of sea salt, lime juice, ginger, cilantro, and honey.
4. Puree everything until it is smooth.
5. Add two pieces of ice to your serving dish and top the ice with an even amount of gazpacho.
6. Garnish the gazpacho with the green onions and some lime pieces.
7. Enjoy.

Hot
Gazpacho

🥣 Prep Time: 15 mins
🕐 Total Time: 25 mins

Servings per Recipe: 8
Calories	115.4
Fat	5.6g
Cholesterol	0.0mg
Sodium	536.8mg
Carbohydrates	15.5g
Protein	2.8g

Ingredients

3 tbsps extra virgin olive oil
3/4 C. chopped red onion
3/4 C. chopped red bell pepper
3/4 C. chopped green bell pepper
3 large garlic cloves, diced
2 C. organic tomato juice
2 C. spicy vegetable juice
1 C. Clamato juice
1 C. organic chicken broth

3 tbsps parsley
3 tbsps basil
3 tbsps chives
kosher sea salt & freshly ground black pepper
2 C. seeded diced fresh tomatoes
1 cucumbers, diced

Directions

1. Begin to stir fry your garlic, onion, and bell peppers for 10 mins.
2. Then combine in the chives, tomato juice, basil, v-8, chicken broth, and clamato.
3. Stir the mix then add in some black pepper and salt.
4. Get everything boiling then shut the heat and combine in the cucumber and tomatoes.
5. Stir the mix again then place the gazpacho in a bowl and place a covering of plastic on the bowl.
6. Put everything in the fridge for 8 hrs.
7. Now stir the gazpacho again and divide the mix between serving dishes.
8. Top each dish with croutons and cheese.
9. Enjoy.

SOUTH AMERICAN
Gazpacho

Prep Time: 10 mins
Total Time: 15 mins

Servings per Recipe: 6	
Calories	378.5
Fat	36.5g
Cholesterol	0.0mg
Sodium	619.8mg
Carbohydrates	12.7g
Protein	2.6g

Ingredients

2 lbs tomatoes, stems removed, cleaned
1 garlic clove, peeled
1/2 an onion, white, diced and peeled
1 green sweet pepper, rinsed, diced,
seed removed
1 cucumber, about 6-7 inches long,
peeled
1/4 tsp ground cumin
3 tbsps red wine vinegar

1/2 tbsp salt
1 C. virgin olive oil
1 piece French bread

Directions

1. Let your bread sit submerged in water for 5 mins then remove the liquids and squeeze the bread to drain more water from it.
2. Add the following to the bowl of a food processor: moist bread, tomatoes, cucumber, garlic, pepper, and onions.
3. Pulse the mix until everything is smooth and all the pieces are small, then add in the cumin, vinegar, salt, French bread (broken into pieces), and olive oil.
4. Pulse everything again until it is creamy.
5. Place everything in a bowl and put the mix in the fridge until it is chilled.
6. Enjoy.

Garlic
Crouton Gazpacho

Prep Time: 15 mins
Total Time: 30 mins

Servings per Recipe: 4
Calories	261.1
Fat	21.1g
Cholesterol	0.0mg
Sodium	73.2mg
Carbohydrates	16.7g
Protein	2.9g

Ingredients

2 red bell peppers, seeded and coarsely chopped
1 cucumber, peeled, seeded, and coarsely chopped
14 oz. tomatoes, large and juicy ones, skinned, seeded and coarsely chopped
4 tbsps olive oil
2 tbsps sherry wine vinegar
salt and pepper
Garlic Croutons
2 tbsps olive oil

1 garlic clove, halved
2 slices bread, crusts removed and cut into 1/4 inch cubes
sea salt
diced green and red bell pepper
chopped seeded cucumber
chopped scallion
ice cube

Directions

1. Add the following to the bowl of a food processor: vinegar, bell peppers, olive oil, tomatoes, and cucumbers.
2. Puree the mix then add in some pepper and salt.
3. Place everything in a bowl and place a covering of plastic on the bowl.
4. Place it all in the fridge for 5 hrs.
5. At the same time begin to stir fry your garlic in oil for 3 mins then remove the garlic from the oil and add in the pieces of bread.
6. Fry the bread until is gold all over then place the pieces on some paper towel to drain.
7. Top the bread with some sea salt and place the pieces in a container.
8. Once the gazpacho is chilled get your bowls for serving and add 2 ice cubes to each one and evenly divide your gazpacho between the bowls.
9. Top everything with the croutons.
10. Enjoy.

CLASSICAL
Gazpacho

Prep Time: 20 mins
Total Time: 2 hrs 20 mins

Servings per Recipe: 10

Calories	39 kcal
Fat	0.2 g
Carbohydrates	< 9.2g
Protein	1.6 g
Cholesterol	0 mg
Sodium	305 mg

Ingredients

4 C. tomato juice
1 onion, diced
1 green bell pepper, diced
1 cucumber, chopped
2 C. chopped tomatoes
2 green onions, chopped
1 clove garlic, diced
3 tbsps fresh lemon juice
2 tbsps red wine vinegar

1 tsp dried tarragon
1 tsp dried basil
1/4 C. chopped fresh parsley
1 tsp white sugar
salt and pepper to taste

Directions

1. Add the following to the bowl of a food processor: black pepper, tomato juice, salt, onion, sugar, bell peppers, parsley, cucumber, basil, tomatoes, tarragon, green onions, wine vinegar, lemon juice, and garlic.
2. Stir the mix evenly then place everything into a bowl and place a covering of plastic on the bowl.
3. Put everything in the fridge for 3 hrs. Enjoy.

Verde
Gazpacho

🥣 Prep Time: 25 mins
🕐 Total Time: 55 mins

Servings per Recipe: 2
Calories   276 kcal
Fat   15.1 g
Carbohydrates   36.3g
Protein   5.1 g
Cholesterol   0 mg
Sodium   47 mg

Ingredients

2 C. diced honeydew melon
1 English (seedless) cucumber, peeled and diced
1 small onion, diced
1 avocado - peeled, pitted, and chopped
1 jalapeno pepper, seeded and coarsely chopped

1 clove garlic, chopped
1/4 C. white balsamic vinegar
1 tbsp lime juice
salt and freshly ground black pepper to taste

Directions

1. Add the following to the bowl of a food processor and puree the mix: black pepper, honeydew, salt, cucumber, lime juice, onion, balsamic vinegar, avocado, garlic, and jalapeno.

2. Puree the mix until it is smooth then add in some pepper and salt.

3. Enjoy.

ARTISAN
Gazpacho

Prep Time: 20 mins
Total Time: 20 mins

Servings per Recipe: 12
Calories	322 kcal
Fat	11.2 g
Carbohydrates	29.1g
Protein	27.1 g
Cholesterol	221 mg
Sodium	948 mg

Ingredients

64 fluid oz. tomato and clam juice cocktail
3 lbs cooked shrimp, peeled and deveined
4 avocados, peeled and chopped
2 cucumbers, cubed
3 large tomatoes, diced
1 red onion, diced
1 bunch cilantro, chopped

2 tbsps lemon juice
1/2 tsp salt
1/4 tsp pepper

Directions

1. Get a bowl, combine: pepper, tomato, salt, clam juice, cilantro, shrimp, red onions, avocados, tomatoes, lemon juice, and cucumbers.

2. Place a covering of plastic on the bowl, and put everything in the fridge until chilled.

3. Enjoy.

Countryside
Gazpacho

🥣 Prep Time: 30 mins
🕐 Total Time: 3 hrs 30 mins

Servings per Recipe: 8
Calories   287 kcal
Fat   23.1 g
Carbohydrates   21g
Protein   4.5 g
Cholesterol   0 mg
Sodium   392 mg

Ingredients

2 1/2 C. tomato-vegetable juice cocktail
2 1/2 C. vegetable broth
3 large tomatoes, diced
3 large avocados - peeled, pitted, and cut into bite-sized pieces
1 C. diced cucumber
1 (8 oz.) can chopped tomatoes with juice
1/2 C. chopped green bell pepper
1/2 C. chopped red bell pepper

1/4 C. extra-virgin olive oil
3 green onions, thinly sliced
1 lemon, juiced, or more to taste
2 tbsps diced fresh cilantro
2 tbsps white wine vinegar
1 dash hot sauce
salt and ground black pepper to taste

Directions

1. Get a bowl, combine: black pepper, tomato juice, salt, broth, hot sauce, tomatoes, avocados, vinegar, cucumber, cilantro, canned tomatoes and liquid, lemon juice, bell peppers, green onions, and olive oil.
2. Place a covering of plastic on the bowl and put everything in the fridge for 4 hrs.
3. Enjoy.

BALSAMIC
Gazpacho

Prep Time: 25 mins
Total Time: 1 hr 25 mins

Servings per Recipe: 6
Calories	58 kcal
Fat	2 g
Carbohydrates	10.9 g
Protein	2 g
Cholesterol	0 mg
Sodium	330 mg

Ingredients

6 medium ripe tomatoes, diced
2 cucumbers, peeled and finely
chopped
1 onion, diced
1 green bell pepper, diced
jalapeno pepper, seeded and diced
1 large lemon, juiced
1 tbsp balsamic vinegar
2 tsps olive oil

1 tsp kosher salt
1/2 tsp ground black pepper
1/4 C. chopped fresh dill

Directions

1. Get a bowl, combine: jalapeno, tomatoes, bell peppers, cucumber, and onions.
2. Stir the mix then add in the pepper, lemon juice, salt, balsamic and olive oil.
3. Stir the mix again then add half of the mix to the bowl of a food processor and puree it then combine in the rest of the gazpacho and puree it as well.
4. Enjoy.

Avocado and Garlic Gazpacho

🥣 Prep Time: 20 mins
🕐 Total Time: 1 hr 20 mins

Servings per Recipe: 4
Calories   155 kcal
Fat   7.9 g
Carbohydrates   19.4g
Protein   4 g
Cholesterol   0 mg
Sodium   248 mg

Ingredients

2 C. shredded zucchini
1 onion, coarsely chopped
1 avocado - peeled, pitted, and coarsely chopped
1/2 C. canned garbanzo beans, drained
1/4 C. apple cider vinegar
1 jalapeno pepper, seeded and diced

2 tsps lemon juice
1 clove garlic, smashed
1/4 tsp salt, or more to taste
1/4 tsp ground black pepper, or more to taste

Directions

1. Get a bowl, combine: black pepper, zucchini, salt, onion, garlic, avocado, garbanzo, lemon juice, apple cider, and jalapenos.
2. Stir the mix then place a covering of plastic on the bowl.
3. Put everything in the fridge for 60 mins.
4. Enjoy.

SOUTHERN
Gazpacho

Prep Time: 20 mins
Total Time: 2 hrs 20 mins

Servings per Recipe: 6

Calories	63 kcal
Fat	2.5 g
Carbohydrates	10.6g
Protein	1.9 g
Cholesterol	0 mg
Sodium	132 mg

Ingredients

5 C. shredded green cabbage
1/2 C. chopped cucumber
1 C. chopped tomato
1/2 C. chopped yellow bell pepper
1/2 C. chopped green onions
1/2 C. chopped celery
1/4 C. tomato-vegetable juice cocktail
1/4 C. red wine vinegar
1 tsp white sugar

1 tbsp olive oil
1 tbsp salsa
1/2 lemon, juiced
salt and pepper to taste

Directions

1. Get a bowl, combine: celery, cabbage, green onions, cucumbers, bell peppers, and tomatoes.
2. Get a 2nd bowl, combine: lemon juice, tomato juice, salsa, vinegar, olive oil, and sugar.
3. Stir in some pepper and salt.
4. Combine both bowls then place a covering of plastic on the bowl and put everything in the fridge for 3 hrs. Enjoy.

Sunrise
Gazpacho

Prep Time: 30 mins
Total Time: 2 hrs 30 mins

Servings per Recipe: 6
Calories	231 kcal
Fat	12.4 g
Carbohydrates	31.4g
Protein	4.2 g
Cholesterol	0 mg
Sodium	605 mg

Ingredients

3 pints hulled strawberries
1/2 cucumber - peeled, seeded, and chopped
1/2 onion, chopped
1/4 C. chopped fresh cilantro
1/4 C. chopped fresh parsley
1 pint hulled strawberries, chopped
1/2 cucumber - peeled, seeded, and chopped
1/2 onion, chopped
1/4 C. chopped fresh cilantro
1/4 C. chopped fresh parsley
1 bunch green onions, diced

1 jalapeno pepper, seeded and diced
1/3 C. red wine vinegar
3 tbsps fresh lemon juice
2 tbsps olive oil
1 1/2 tsps salt
2 cloves garlic, diced
1 tsp dried tarragon
1 tsp dried basil
1/4 tsp hot pepper sauce
1/8 tsp ground black pepper
1 large avocado - peeled, pitted, and cubed

Directions

1. Add the following to the bowl of a food processor: 1/4 C. parsley, 3 pints strawberries, 1/4 C. cilantro, half of the onion, half of the cucumber.
2. Process the mix for 1 min then place everything in a bowl.
3. Now add the following to the pureed mix: black pepper, 1 pint strawberries, hot sauce, 1/2 cucumber, basil, tarragon, 1/2 onion, garlic, salt, 1/4 C. cilantro, olive oil, 1/4 C. parsley, lemon juice, wine vinegar, jalapenos, and green onions.
4. Top everything with the pieces of avocado then place a covering of plastic on the bowl and put the mix in the fridge for 3 hrs.
5. Enjoy.

PARSLEY
Gazpacho

Prep Time: 20 mins
Total Time: 1 hr 10 mins

Servings per Recipe: 6
Calories   210 kcal
Fat   13.2 g
Carbohydrates   12.6g
Protein   11.7 g
Cholesterol   27 mg
Sodium   587 mg

Ingredients

1 (1 lb) package bacon, cut into 1-inch pieces
8 large ripe tomatoes, diced
1/2 salad cucumber, diced
1 onion, chopped
1 tbsp extra-virgin olive oil

1 clove garlic, diced
1/4 tsp dried parsley, or to taste
salt and ground black pepper to taste

Directions

1. Stir fry your bacon for 12 mins until fully done then place the bacon to the side and crumble it.
2. Add the onion, cucumber, and tomatoes to a bowl of a food processor and puree the mix.
3. Now begin to stir fry your garlic for 60 mins in olive oil then add the pureed mix to the oil.
4. Stir everything then add in the pepper, salt, and parsley and stir everything again.
5. Place a lid on the pan, set the heat to low, and let the contents cook for 1 hr.
6. Top the gazpacho with the bacon.
7. Enjoy.

Maggie's
Favorite Gazpacho

🥘 Prep Time: 10 mins
🕐 Total Time: 1 hr 10 mins

Servings per Recipe: 7
Calories	301 kcal
Fat	9.4 g
Carbohydrates	46.5g
Protein	9.8 g
Cholesterol	0 mg
Sodium	553 mg

Ingredients

8 C. cold water
8 large tomatoes - peeled, seeded and chopped
1/4 C. diced onion
1 clove garlic, diced
1 cucumber, peeled and finely chopped
1 green bell pepper, diced

1 (1 lb) loaf stale French bread, cut into 1 inch cubes
1/4 C. olive oil
1/4 C. wine vinegar
1/8 tbsp salt

Directions

1. Add the following to a big pot: oil, water, bread, and tomatoes.
2. Add the green pepper, onions, cucumbers, and garlic to the bowl of a food processor and puree the mix.
3. Add the puree to the pot. With a hand blender, blend the mix until it is smooth, then combine in some salt and the vinegar.
4. Enjoy.

ORANGE
and Watermelon Gazpacho

Prep Time: 10 mins
Total Time: 1 hr 10 mins

Servings per Recipe: 6

Calories	110 kcal
Fat	4.8 g
Carbohydrates	16.4g
Protein	1.8 g
Cholesterol	0 mg
Sodium	3 mg

Ingredients

2 C. 1/4-inch-diced watermelon
2 C. orange juice
2 tbsps extra-virgin olive oil
1 seedless cucumber, cut into 1/4-inch dice
1 small yellow bell pepper, seeded and cut into 1/4-inch dice
1 small onion, cut into 1/4-inch dice
2 medium garlic cloves, diced

1 small jalapeno pepper, seeded and diced (optional)
3 tbsps fresh lime juice
2 tbsps chopped fresh parsley, basil or cilantro
Salt and freshly ground black pepper

Directions

1. Pure the oil, orange juice, and watermelon until smooth then place everything in a bowl.
2. Add in the cucumbers, bell peppers, onion, garlic, jalapenos, lime juice, parsley, and some pepper and salt.
3. Stir the mix then place a covering of plastic on the bowl.
4. Put everything in the fridge until it is chilled.
5. Enjoy.

Hawaiian
Gazpacho

Prep Time: 10 mins
Total Time: 1 hr 10 mins

Servings per Recipe: 6
Calories	130 kcal
Fat	4.8 g
Carbohydrates	22.2g
Protein	1.2 g
Cholesterol	0 mg
Sodium	5 mg

Ingredients

2 C. fresh pineapple in 1/4-inch dice
2 C. pineapple juice
2 tbsps extra virgin olive oil
1 seedless cucumber, cut into 1/4-inch dice
1 small red bell pepper, seeded and cut into 1/4-inch dice
1 small onion, cut into 1/4-inch dice
2 medium garlic cloves, diced

1 small jalapeno pepper, seeded and diced (optional)
3 tbsps fresh lime juice
2 tbsps chopped fresh parsley, basil or cilantro
Salt and freshly ground black pepper

Directions

1. Puree the oil and half a C. of pineapple with liquid until smooth then place the mix in a bowl.
2. Add the rest of the pineapple, the fresh pineapple, cucumber, bell peppers, onion, garlic, jalapenos, lime juice, parsley, some black pepper, and salt.
3. Stir the mix then place a covering of plastic on the bowl.
4. Put everything in the fridge until chilled.
5. Enjoy.

GAZPACHO
from Spain

Prep Time: 30 mins
Total Time: 4 hrs 30 mins

Servings per Recipe: 10
Calories	140 kcal
Fat	3.3 g
Carbohydrates	23.1g
Protein	6.7 g
Cholesterol	0 mg
Sodium	709 mg

Ingredients

1 cucumber, peeled and diced
1 green bell pepper, diced
5 green onions, chopped
2 cloves garlic, diced
3 tomatoes, diced
2 stalks celery, diced
2 1/2 C. navy beans, rinsed and drained
2 tbsps olive oil
6 tbsps red wine vinegar

1 (46 fluid oz.) can tomato juice
1 tsp ground cumin
1 tbsp diced fresh parsley
1 tbsp diced fresh basil
1/2 tbsp diced fresh oregano
1/4 tsp salt

Directions

1. Get a bowl, combine: tomato juice, salt, cumin, oregano, basil, parsley, cucumber, vinegar, bell peppers, olive oil, green onions, navy beans, garlic, celery, and tomatoes.
2. Stir the mix then place a covering of plastic on the bowl.
3. Put everything in the fridge 5 hrs. Enjoy.

Jalapeno
Gazpacho

Prep Time: 10 mins
Total Time: 1 hr 20 mins

Servings per Recipe: 6
Calories	85 kcal
Fat	4.6 g
Carbohydrates	8.1g
Protein	1.7 g
Cholesterol	0 mg
Sodium	215 mg

Ingredients

2 (14.5 oz.) cans diced tomatoes
1/2 C. water
2 tbsps extra-virgin olive oil
1 seedless cucumber, cut into 1/4-inch dice
1 small yellow bell pepper, seeded and cut into 1/4-inch dice
1 small onion, cut into 1/4-inch dice
2 medium garlic cloves, diced

1 small jalapeno pepper, seeded and diced (optional)
2 tbsps sherry vinegar
2 tbsps chopped fresh parsley, basil or cilantro
Salt and freshly ground black pepper

Directions

1. Puree the oil, water, and half a C. of tomatoes until smooth then place the mix in bowl.
2. Add in the cucumber, bell peppers, onions, the rest of the tomatoes, garlic, jalapeno, vinegar, parsley, some pepper and salt.
3. Stir the mix then place a covering of plastic on the bowl and put everything in the fridge for 60 mins.
4. Enjoy.

SUMMER
Solstice Gazpacho

Prep Time: 15 mins
Total Time: 3 hrs 15 mins

Servings per Recipe: 4
Calories	166 kcal
Fat	4.9 g
Carbohydrates	27.9 g
Protein	4.2 g
Cholesterol	0 mg
Sodium	476 mg

Ingredients

1 (24 oz.) jar Tomato and Basil Sauce
24 oz. water
3 tbsps fresh lemon juice
2 tbsps granulated sugar
Hot pepper sauce, to taste
1 tbsp extra-virgin olive oil
1 medium fresh tomato, chopped
1/2 C. chopped red bell pepper
1/2 C. chopped yellow bell pepper

1/4 C. diced red onion
1 1/2 C. diced English cucumber
1/4 C. chopped fresh basil
Salt and freshly ground black pepper, to taste
Fresh chopped parsley, for garnish (optional)

Directions

1. Get a bowl, mix: olive oil, tomato sauce, hot sauce, water, sugar, and lemon juice.
2. Combine in the cucumber, tomato, red onion, and bell peppers.
3. Stir the mix then add in some pepper, salt, and the basil.
4. Place a covering of plastic on the bowl and put everything in the fridge for 4 hrs.
5. Enjoy.

Crab
Gazpacho

Prep Time: 30 mins
Total Time: 8 hrs 30 mins

Servings per Recipe: 4
Calories	440 kcal
Fat	8.4 g
Carbohydrates	72.8g
Protein	19.3 g
Cholesterol	116 mg
Sodium	2297 mg

Ingredients

1 (64 oz.) bottle tomato and clam juice cocktail
1/4 C. ketchup
lemons, juiced
1 tbsp chopped fresh cilantro
1 large cucumber, seeded and diced
1/2 lb cooked small shrimp

4 oz. imitation crabmeat, chopped
1 green bell pepper, chopped (optional)
1 avocado - peeled, pitted, and diced
1 tomato, diced

Directions

1. Get a bowl, combine: bell peppers, cocktail juice, tomato, crabmeat, ketchup, shrimp, lemon juice, cucumber, and cilantro.
2. Stir the mix then place a covering of plastic on the bowl.
3. Put everything in the fridge overnight then divide the gazpacho between serving dishes.
4. Top each one with some tomato and avocado pieces.
5. Enjoy.

WESTERN EUROPEAN
Gazpacho

Prep Time: 20 mins
Total Time: 1 hr 20 mins

Servings per Recipe: 4

Calories	329 kcal
Fat	28.3 g
Carbohydrates	18.2g
Protein	3.5 g
Cholesterol	0 mg
Sodium	830 mg

Ingredients

3/4 green bell pepper, seeded
1/2 cucumber, peeled and sliced
2 cloves garlic, chopped
1/2 C. olive oil
2 day-old crusty bread rolls, cut into
thick slices

6 tomatoes, peeled and quartered
1/2 tbsp kosher salt
1 pinch cayenne pepper
1/2 tsp balsamic vinegar
1/4 tsp olive oil

Directions

1. Add the following to the bowl of a food processor: 1/2 C. olive oil, bell peppers, garlic, and cucumber.
2. Puree the mix then combine in the bread gradually.
3. Continue to puree each piece of bread into the mix then add in the tomatoes slowly as well.
4. Puree the entire mix then place everything in a bowl. Stir in the cayenne and salt then place a covering of plastic on the bowl.
5. Put everything in the fridge for 60 mins then top the gazpacho with 1/4 tsp olive oil and the balsamic vinegar. Enjoy.

Latin
Gazpacho

Prep Time: 15 mins
Total Time: 15 mins

Servings per Recipe: 4
Calories	197 kcal
Fat	14.7 g
Carbohydrates	16.1g
Protein	3.2 g
Cholesterol	0 mg
Sodium	19 mg

Ingredients

10 ripe tomatoes, quartered
1/2 red onion, diced
1 serrano chile pepper, seeded and diced
1/2 C. chopped fresh cilantro, or to taste
2 limes, juiced
3 cloves garlic, peeled

1 tsp red wine vinegar, or to taste
salt to taste
1/4 C. extra-virgin olive oil (optional)

Directions

1. Add the following to the bowl of a food processor: serrano, red onions, and tomatoes.
2. Puree the mix then combine in the salt, cilantro, vinegar, garlic, and lime juice.
3. Puree the mix again then add in the olive oil in a slow stream as you run the machine with a low heat.
4. Puree the gazpacho until it is smooth again then place everything in a serving bowl.
5. Enjoy.

NEW WORLD
Ceviche

Prep Time: 1 hr
Total Time: 9 hrs

Servings per Recipe: 20

Calories	152 kcal
Fat	4.9 g
Carbohydrates	19.7g
Protein	8.3 g
Cholesterol	49 mg
Sodium	597 mg

Ingredients

1 (16 oz.) package cooked medium shrimp, peeled and deveined
2 (8 oz.) packages imitation crabmeat, cut into 1-inch pieces
5 tomatoes, diced
3 avocados, peeled and diced
1 English cucumber, peeled and cut into bite-size pieces
1 red onion, diced
1 bunch cilantro, chopped, or more to taste

4 limes, juiced
2 jalapeno peppers, seeded and finely diced
2 cloves garlic, pressed
1 (64 oz.) bottle tomato and clam juice cocktail
salt and ground black pepper to taste

Directions

1. Get a bowl, combine: garlic, crab, jalapeno, tomatoes, lime juice, avocados, shrimp, cilantro, cucumber, and red onions.
2. Stir the mix then add in the clam juice cocktail.
3. Stir the mix again then place a covering of plastic on the bowl and put everything in the fridge for 8 hrs.
4. Enjoy.

Gazpacho
Appetizer

🥣 Prep Time: 5 mins

🕐 Total Time: 5 mins

Servings per Recipe: 20
Calories	12.1
Fat	0.8g
Cholesterol	0.0mg
Sodium	49.2mg
Carbohydrates	1.1g
Protein	0.1g

Ingredients

1 C. tomatoes, chopped
1/4 C. red onion, chopped
1/2 C. green bell pepper, chopped
1/2 C. cucumber, chopped

1/4 C. Italian dressing

Directions

1. Get a bowl, combine: tomatoes, red onions, bell peppers, cucumber, and Italian dressing.
2. Stir the mix then place a covering of plastic on the bowl.
3. Put everything in the fridge for 60 mins.
4. Enjoy.

SHERRY
Gazpacho

Prep Time: 20 mins
Total Time: 20 mins

Servings per Recipe: 4
Calories   55.4
Fat   3.6g
Cholesterol   0.0mg
Sodium   396.9mg
Carbohydrates   5.8g
Protein   1.1g

Ingredients

1 cucumber, peeled, seeded, and chopped
1 large tomatoes, ripe chopped
1/2 C. roasted red pepper, jarred chopped
1 celery rib, chopped
1 garlic clove, diced

1 tbsp extra virgin olive oil
1/2 tbsp sherry wine vinegar
1 tsp lemon juice
1/4 tsp salt
1/8 tsp pepper

Directions

1. Get a bowl, combine: cucumber, tomatoes, red peppers, celery, garlic, olive oil, vinegar, lemon juice, salt, and pepper.
2. Stir the mix, then place a covering of plastic on the bowl.
3. Put everything in the fridge for 60 mins.
4. Enjoy.

Gazpacho
Chiller

Prep Time: 15 mins
Total Time: 15 mins

Servings per Recipe: 6
Calories	26.8
Fat	0.1g
Cholesterol	0.0mg
Sodium	222.2mg
Carbohydrates	6.1g
Protein	1.1g

Ingredients

1 1/4 C. chopped tomatoes
3/4 C. coarsely chopped peeled English cucumber
1/4 C. chopped sweet green pepper
2 tbsps chopped onions
1 clove garlic, smashed
2 C. tomato juice

2 tbsps red wine vinegar or 2 tbsps cider vinegar
1/4 tsp dried dill
1 dash hot pepper sauce
pepper
alfalfa sprout

Directions

1. Add the following to the bowl of a food processor: garlic, tomatoes, onion, cucumber, and green pepper. Puree the mix, then add in some pepper, some salt, the tomato juice, hot sauce, dill weed, and the vinegar. Puree the mix again then place everything in a bowl covered with plastic.
2. Put the gazpacho in the fridge for 60 mins then divide the dish between serving bowls.
3. Top each serving with some alfalfa. Enjoy.

MANHATTAN
Gazpacho

Prep Time: 30 mins
Total Time: 45 mins

Servings per Recipe: 10
Calories   88.2
Fat   7 g
Cholesterol   0.0mg
Sodium   586.2mg
Carbohydrates   6.4g
Protein   1.1g

Ingredients

8 plum tomatoes, diced
1 1/2 cucumbers, skin removed, diced
1 1/2 onions, skin removed, diced
1 1/2 bell peppers, cut into 4 pieces
3 garlic cloves, skin removed, diced
3 tbsps red wine vinegar
5 tbsps olive oil

2 1/2 tsps salt
1/2 tsp black pepper

Directions

1. Get a bowl, combine: tomatoes, cucumbers, onions, bell peppers, and garlic.

2. Stir the mix to distribute the garlic then add in the black pepper and salt.

3. Stir the mix again then stir in the olive oil and vinegar.

4. Combine everything evenly then place a covering of plastic on the bowl and put everything in the fridge for 25 mins.

5. Enjoy

Green
Spanish Gazpacho

Prep Time: 20 mins
Total Time: 21 mins

Servings per Recipe: 4
Calories	69.0
Fat	3.7g
Cholesterol	0.0mg
Sodium	182.6mg
Carbohydrates	8.8g
Protein	2.3g

Ingredients

1 quart water
4 oz. fresh spinach, washed and dried in a spinner
3 scallions, trimmed and roughly chopped
1/4 C. loosely packed fresh parsley leaves
4 fresh nasturtium leaves
3 large fresh basil leaves
1 cucumber, roughly chopped
1 tbsp extra virgin olive oil
1 large garlic clove, chopped

2 tbsps fresh lime juice
1 1/2 C. vegetable stock
1/4 tsp salt
fresh ground black pepper
1 scallion, white and green parts, diced
1 cucumber, finely diced
thin slices lime

Directions

1. Get 2 pieces of diced scallion boiling with the spinach for 2 mins then remove all the liquids.
2. Place everything in the blender besides the cucumber, remaining scallions, and pepper and salt.
3. Puree the rest of the ingredients then add in the cucumber and remaining scallions.
4. Puree the mix again then place everything in a bowl.
5. Place a covering of plastic on the bowl and put the mix in the fridge for 2 hrs.
6. Enjoy.

PASTA
Gazpacho

Prep Time: 20 mins
Total Time: 30 mins

Servings per Recipe: 6
Calories	111.6
Fat	0.8g
Cholesterol	0.0mg
Sodium	39.5mg
Carbohydrates	22.4g
Protein	3.9g

Ingredients

4 oz. uncooked macaroni
2 1/2 C. tomatoes, seeded and chopped
1 C. red onion, diced
1 C. cucumber, diced
1/2 C. celery, diced
1/2 C. green bell pepper, diced
1/2 C. red bell pepper, diced
2 tbsps black olives, diced
3 tbsps cider vinegar
1 bay leaf
2 tbsps fresh parsley, diced

1 tbsp fresh thyme, diced
1 garlic clove, diced
3 - 4 dashes hot pepper sauce
1/4 tsp ground black pepper
whole olive
sliced cucumber
dill sprigs

Directions

1. Get your pasta boiling in water and salt for 9 mins then remove all the liquids.
2. Get a bowl and mix the pasta with all the ingredients.
3. Place a covering of plastic on the bowl and put the gazpacho in the fridge for 5 hrs.
4. Add in any garnishes.
5. Enjoy.

Ripe
Gazpacho

Prep Time: 10 mins
Total Time: 45 mins

Servings per Recipe: 4
Calories   297.4
Fat   19.2g
Cholesterol   0.0mg
Sodium   134.5mg
Carbohydrates   30.0g
Protein   5.4g

Ingredients

4 ripe tomatoes
2 small eggplants or 1 medium eggplant,
peeled and cut into large chunks
4 small zucchini or 2 medium zucchini,
but into large chunks
2 medium onions, cut into large chunks
10 garlic cloves, peeled
1/2 C. extra virgin olive oil
1/2 C. sherry wine vinegar
salt

ground black pepper
4 C. water
4 slices stale bread, crusts removed and torn
up
crouton

Directions

1. Set your oven to 400 degrees before doing anything else.
2. Add the following to a casserole dish in the oven: olive oil, garlic, onions, tomatoes, zucchini, and eggplant.
3. Roast everything for 35 mins then enter everything into a bowl.
4. Add in the bread, vinegar, water, pepper, and salt.
5. Stir the mix then place a covering of covering of plastic on the bowl and put everything in the fridge for 2 hrs.
6. Now enter the contents into a food processor and puree it.
7. Enjoy.

MEXICAN
Gazpacho

Prep Time: 30 mins
Total Time: 40 mins

Servings per Recipe: 12
Calories   473.6
Fat   8.8g
Cholesterol   0.0mg
Sodium   1609.5mg
Carbohydrates   83.0g
Protein   23.5g

Ingredients

7 (16 oz.) cans black beans, drained
2 (4 oz.) jars capers, drained
1 large raw yellow onion, grated
1 small raw yellow onion, grated
3 (4 oz.) jars sliced pimientos, drained, rinsed
3 tsps cumin
4 tbsps cilantro
3 limes, juice of
3 (8 oz.) cans green chilies, chopped variety

13 C. regular flavor V8 vegetable juice
6 tbsps extra virgin olive oil
6 tbsps Worcestershire sauce
1 1/2 C. garlic
3 tbsps balsamic vinegar
2 (12 oz.) jars medium heat salsa
1 (6 oz.) jars bottle hot salsa
3 large chopped cucumbers

Directions

1. Divide all the ingredients between two large pots then puree them with a hand mixer for 5 mins each.
2. Place everything in a big bowl and place a covering of plastic on the bowl.
3. Put the mix in the fridge for 4 hrs.
4. Enjoy.

Strawberry
Pineapple Gazpacho

Prep Time: 20 mins
Total Time: 25 mins

Servings per Recipe: 4
Calories   109.2
Fat   0.3g
Cholesterol   0.0mg
Sodium   3.6mg
Carbohydrates   27.4g
Protein   1.1g

Ingredients

1/2 C. diced pineapple
1/2 C. diced strawberry
1 C. sliced grapes
3/4 C. blueberries
1 C. apple juice

1/2 C. orange juice
1/4 tsp black pepper
1/2 orange, segmented

Directions

1. Get a bowl, combine: blueberries, pineapple, grapes, and strawberries.
2. Stir the mix then place a covering of plastic on the bowl.
3. Put everything in the fridge until chilled, then divide the mix between serving bowls.
4. Top each serving with the orange and pepper.
5. Enjoy.

EAST COAST
Gazpacho

Prep Time: 30 mins
Total Time: 30 mins

Servings per Recipe: 2
Calories	85.1
Fat	5.3g
Cholesterol	0.0mg
Sodium	639.2mg
Carbohydrates	9.6g
Protein	1.8g

Ingredients

1 C. tomato juice or 1 C. vegetable juice
1/2 C. fresh tomato, peeled, seeded, diced
3 1/4 tbsps celery, diced
3 1/4 tbsps cucumbers, diced
3 1/4 tbsps green bell peppers, diced
3 1/4 tbsps green onions, diced
1 1/4 tbsps white wine vinegar
3/4 tbsp extra virgin olive oil
1/3 large garlic clove, diced
3/4 tsp fresh flat-leaf parsley, diced

1/4 tsp salt
1/4 tsp Worcestershire sauce
1/4 tsp black pepper, freshly ground

Directions

1. Get a bowl, combine: tomato juice, fresh tomato, celery, cucumbers, bell peppers, green onions, vinegar, olive oil, garlic, parsley, salt, Worcestershire, and black pepper.
2. Stir the mix then place a covering of plastic on the bowl.
3. Put everything in the fridge until chilled.
4. Enjoy.

Little Tomato
Gazpacho

🥣 Prep Time: 20 mins
🕐 Total Time: 25 mins

Servings per Recipe: 4
Calories   296.6
Fat   23.4g
Cholesterol   0.0mg
Sodium   344.8mg
Carbohydrates   21.1g
Protein   6.1g

Ingredients

1 (14 oz.) cans chicken broth
1 lb tomatillo, quartered
1 garlic clove, diced
2 tbsps extra virgin olive oil
2 medium avocados, finely diced
1 small cucumber, seeded and finely diced
1 red bell pepper, finely diced

1/4 small red onion, finely diced
2 tbsps fresh cilantro, chopped
1 tbsp fresh lime juice
kosher salt, to taste
fresh ground black pepper, to taste

Directions

1. Get your garlic and tomatillos boiling in the broth.
2. Once the mix is boiling set the heat to low, and let the contents gently cook for 3 mins.
3. Now shut the heat and let everything cool.
4. Once the mix is boiling use an immersion blender to puree the mix then add in the olive and puree everything again.
5. Add in some pepper and salt then place everything in a bowl and place a covering of plastic on the bowl.
6. Put the mix in the fridge until cold.
7. Enjoy.

FRENCH STYLE
Gazpacho

Prep Time: 20 mins
Total Time: 35 mins

Servings per Recipe: 4
Calories   179.4
Fat   4.8g
Cholesterol   0.0mg
Sodium   560.4mg
Carbohydrates   31.0g
Protein   5.5g

Ingredients

4 oz. French bread, cut into 1/2-inch cubes
olive oil flavored cooking spray
4 C. tomatoes, seeded and chopped
2 C. boneless skinless chicken breasts
2 C. cucumbers, seeded, chopped
1 C. chopped green bell pepper
1/2 C. chopped red bell pepper
1/2 C. red onion, diced
1/3 C. chopped fresh flat leaf parsley
1/2 C. V8 vegetable juice

1/4 C. red wine vinegar
1 tbsp extra virgin olive oil
1 tbsp water
3 garlic cloves, diced
1/2 tsp salt
1/8 tsp pepper

Directions

1. Set your oven to 350 degrees before doing anything else.
2. Toast your bread in the oven after coating them with olive oil, on a cookie sheet, for 20 mins.
3. Get a bowl, combine: parsley, tomato, onion, chicken, bell peppers, and cucumbers.
4. Get a 2nd bowl, combine: pepper, veggie juice, salt, vinegar, garlic, water, and olive oil.
5. Combine both bowls then stir the mix.
6. Add in the toasted bread and stir the mix again.
7. Enjoy.

Cha-Cha
Gazpacho

Prep Time: 45 mins
Total Time: 50 mins

Servings per Recipe: 18
Calories   54.8
Fat   0.3g
Cholesterol   0.0mg
Sodium   433.8mg
Carbohydrates   12.6g
Protein   1.8g

Ingredients

3 C. zucchini, diced
3 C. cucumbers, diced
1 1/2 C. red onions, diced
4 C. sweet peppers, diced
7 garlic cloves
8 C. vegetable cocktail

1 1/2 C. taco sauce
1 C. balsamic vinegar
1 tbsp honey
hot sauce

Directions

1. Chop all the veggies.
2. Get a bowl, combine: honey, cocktail juice, balsamic, and taco sauce.
3. Add in the veggies and serve the dish.
4. Enjoy.

LOUISIANA
Gazpacho

Prep Time: 25 mins
Total Time: 1 hr 25 mins

Servings per Recipe: 20
Calories	58.8
Fat	3.6g
Cholesterol	0.0mg
Sodium	118.6mg
Carbohydrates	6.4g
Protein	1.3g

Ingredients

10 C. ripe tomatoes, peeled and diced
3 C. cucumbers, peeled and quartered
1/2 C. yellow bell pepper, diced
1/2 C. celery, chopped
3 C. tomato juice
5 tbsps olive oil
3 tbsps vinegar

3 tbsps garlic, diced
3 tbsps Tabasco sauce
2 tbsps lemon juice
2 tbsps creole seasoning

Directions

1. Add the following to the bowl of a food processor: onion, tomatoes, bell peppers, and cucumbers.
2. Get a bowl, and add in the pureed mix and the rest of the ingredients.
3. Stir the mix then place a covering of plastic on the bowl.
4. Put everything in the fridge for 2 hrs.
5. Enjoy.

Maiz
Gazpacho

Prep Time: 15 mins
Total Time: 1 hr 15 mins

Servings per Recipe: 4
Calories	93.9
Fat	0.0mg
Cholesterol	791.0mg
Sodium	22.2g
Carbohydrates	3.7g
Protein	3.8 g

Ingredients

1 C. fresh corn, cooked
1 tomatoes, chopped and seeded
3 C. tomato juice
1 cucumber, unpeeled and diced
1/2 C. white onion, diced finely
1/2 jalapeno, seeded and diced
1 garlic clove, diced

2 tbsps fresh basil leaves, diced
3 tbsps fresh lime juice
1/2 tsp salt
1/4 tsp fresh ground black pepper
basil leaves

Directions

1. Get a bowl, combine: corn, tomatoes, tomato juice, cucumber, onion, jalapeno, garlic, basil, lime juice, salt, and black pepper.
2. Stir the mix then garnish the gazpacho with the basil leaves before serving.
3. Enjoy.

AUTHENTIC
Spanish Gazpacho

Prep Time: 20 mins
Total Time: 20 mins

Servings per Recipe: 12

Calories	322 kcal
Carbohydrates	29.1 g
Cholesterol	221 mg
Fat	11.2 g
Protein	27.1 g
Sodium	948 mg

Ingredients

64 fluid ounces tomato and clam juice cocktail
3 pounds cooked shrimp, peeled and deveined
4 avocados, peeled and chopped
2 cucumbers, cubed
3 large tomatoes, diced
1 red onion, diced

1 bunch cilantro, chopped
2 tbsps lemon juice
1/2 tsp salt
1/4 tsp pepper

Directions

1. Combine all the ingredients mentioned above in a large bowl before refrigerating it for at least an hour before serving.

Midtown
Gazpacho

Prep Time: 30 mins
Total Time: 45 mins

Servings per Recipe: 10
Calories   88.2
Cholesterol   0.0mg
Sodium   586.2mg
Carbohydrates   6.4g
Protein   1.1g

Ingredients

8 plum tomatoes, diced
1 1/2 cucumbers, skin removed, diced
1 1/2 onions, skin removed, minced
1 1/2 bell peppers, cut into 4 pieces
3 garlic cloves, skin removed, minced
3 tbsps red wine vinegar
5 tbsps olive oil

2 1/2 tsps salt
1/2 tsp black pepper

Directions

1. Get a bowl, combine: tomatoes, cucumbers, onions, bell peppers, and garlic.
2. Stir the mix to distribute the garlic then add in the black pepper and salt.
3. Stir the mix again then stir in the olive oil and vinegar.
4. Combine everything evenly then place a covering of plastic on the bowl and put everything in the fridge for 25 mins.
5. Enjoy.

MAGGIE'S
Easy Spiralizer Gazpacho

Prep Time: 20 mins

Total Time: 2 hrs 20 mins

Servings per Recipe: 4	
Calories	155 kcal
Fat	7.9 g
Carbohydrates	19.4g
Protein	4 g
Cholesterol	0 mg
Sodium	248 mg

Ingredients

2 C. zucchini, spiralized into thin noodles

1 onion, coarsely diced

1 avocado - peeled, pitted, and coarsely diced

1/2 C. canned garbanzo beans, drained

1/4 C. apple cider vinegar

1 jalapeno pepper, seeded and minced

2 tsps lemon juice (optional)

1 clove garlic, smashed

1/4 tsp salt, or more to taste

1/4 tsp ground black pepper, or more to taste

Directions

1. Get a bowl, combine: pepper, zucchini, garlic, salt, onions, lemon juice, avocado, jalapeno, garbanzos, and cider vinegar.

2. Stir the mix to evenly distribute the contents and place a covering of plastic around the bowl.

3. Put everything in the fridge for 2 hrs.

4. Enjoy.

The Best
Avocado Gazpacho

Prep Time: 20 mins
Total Time: 1 hr 20 mins

Servings per Recipe: 4
Calories	155 kcal
Fat	7.9 g
Carbohydrates	19.4g
Protein	4 g
Cholesterol	0 mg
Sodium	248 mg

Ingredients

2 C. shredded zucchini
1 onion, coarsely chopped
1 avocado, peeled, pitted, and coarsely chopped
1/2 C. canned garbanzo beans, drained
1/4 C. apple cider vinegar
1 jalapeno pepper, seeded and diced

2 tsps lemon juice
1 clove garlic, smashed
1/4 tsp salt, or more to taste
1/4 tsp ground black pepper, or more to taste

Directions

1. Get a bowl, mix: pepper, zucchini, salt, onions, garlic, avocado, lemon juice, garbanzo beans, jalapenos, and cider vinegar.
2. Stir the mix to evenly distribute the ingredients. Then place a covering of plastic on the bowl and put everything in the fridge for 60 mins.
3. Enjoy.

MARIA'S
Gazpacho

Prep Time: 30 mins
Total Time: 3 hrs 30 mins

Servings per Recipe: 8
Calories   287 kcal
Fat   23.1 g
Carbohydrates   21g
Protein   4.5 g
Cholesterol   0 mg
Sodium   392 mg

Ingredients

2 1/2 C. tomato-vegetable juice cocktail
2 1/2 C. vegetable broth
3 large tomatoes, diced
3 large avocados, peeled, pitted, and cut into bite-sized pieces
1 C. diced cucumber
1 (8 oz.) can chopped tomatoes with juice
1/2 C. chopped green bell pepper
1/2 C. chopped red bell pepper

1/4 C. extra-virgin olive oil
3 green onions, thinly sliced
1 lemon, juiced, or more to taste
2 tbsps diced fresh cilantro
2 tbsps white wine vinegar
1 dash hot pepper sauce
salt and ground black pepper to taste

Directions

1. Get a bowl, combine: black pepper, tomato-veggie juice, salt, veggie broth, hot sauce, tomatoes, canned tomatoes and their liquid, vinegar, bell peppers, cilantro, olive oil, cucumbers, avocados, lemon juice, and green onions.

2. Place a covering of plastic on the bowl and put everything in the fridge for 4 hrs.

3. Enjoy.

Gazpacho

Prep Time: 20 mins
Total Time: 20 mins

Servings per Recipe: 12
Calories   322 kcal
Carbohydrates   29.1 g
Cholesterol   221 mg
Fat   11.2 g
Protein   27.1 g
Sodium   948 mg

Ingredients

64 fluid ounces tomato and clam juice cocktail
3 pounds cooked shrimp, peeled and deveined
4 avocados, peeled and chopped
2 cucumbers, cubed
3 large tomatoes, diced

1 red onion, diced
1 bunch cilantro, chopped
2 tbsps lemon juice
1/2 tsp salt
1/4 tsp pepper

Directions

1. Combine all the ingredients mentioned above in a large bowl before refrigerating it for at least an hour before serving.

PANHANDLE
Gazpacho

Prep Time: 30 mins
Total Time: 1 hr 30 mins

Servings per Recipe: 6
Calories   250.5
Cholesterol   95.2mg
Sodium   502.1mg
Carbohydrates   25.8g
Protein   15.3g

Ingredients

3 lbs red ripe tomatoes, peeled, seeded, and coarsely chopped
1 medium green pepper, seeded and coarsely chopped
1 small cucumber, peeled, seeded and coarsely chopped
1 medium red onion, peeled and coarsely chopped
3 green onions, sliced
2 garlic cloves, peeled and coarsely chopped
3 sprigs fresh basil
3 sprigs fresh cilantro
1/4 C. extra virgin olive oil
1 tsp rice wine vinegar
1/4 tsp cayenne pepper
1 pinch oregano
salt, to taste
white pepper, to taste
1 C. fresh corn kernels
1 French baguette, sliced in 12 slices
2 garlic cloves, whole and peeled
1 lb shrimp, steamed, peeled and coarsely chopped and cooled
fresh basil, chopped

Directions

1. Get a bowl, combine: oregano, tomatoes, cayenne, green pepper, basil, rice vinegar, green pepper, olive oil (3 tbsps), cucumber, cilantro, green onions, and garlic.
2. Puree the mix with a blender until it is smooth then place everything back into the bowl add in the white pepper and salt then stir everything.
3. Place a covering of plastic on the bowl and put everything into the fridge for 60 mins.
4. Add a quarter of a C. of water and the corn into a pan and get everything boiling.
5. Let the mix boil for 5 mins then remove any remaining liquids.
6. Now get your oven's broiler hot and place the pieces of bread on a cookie sheet.
7. Place the bread under the broiler until they are crunchy then rub them with the garlic and some olive oil.
8. Add your shrimp to the corn and combine everything into the cucumber mix.
9. Divide the mix between serving bowls and top each with basil and place a piece of bread into each bowl.
10. Enjoy.

Andalusia
Gazpacho

Prep Time: 1 hr
Total Time: 7 hrs

Servings per Recipe: 10
Calories   285
Fat   10.5g
Cholesterol   0mg
Sodium   1967mg
Carbohydrates   44.7g
Protein   5.8g

Ingredients

4 stalks celery, diced
3 red bell peppers, diced
3 yellow bell peppers, diced
2 cucumbers, chopped
4 small avocados - peeled, pitted, and diced
1 bunch cilantro, chopped
1 bunch green onions, diced
1/2 red onion, diced
1 (46 fluid oz.) bottle tomato-vegetable juice cocktail

2 (32 oz.) bottles tomato and clam juice cocktail
1 (12 oz.) bottle hot pepper sauce
1/3 C. red wine vinegar
1/3 C. lemon juice
3 cloves garlic, minced
1 tbsp garlic powder
salt and ground black pepper

Directions

1. In a non-reactive bowl, add all the ingredients and mix until well combined.
2. Place in the fridge for about 6-8 hours.
3. Enjoy Chilled.

ISLAND
Gazpacho

Prep Time: 20 mins
Total Time: 20 mins

Servings per Recipe: 6
Calories	147 kcal
Fat	5 g
Cholesterol	26.2g
Sodium	1.6 g
Carbohydrates	0 mg
Protein	5 mg

Ingredients

2 C. 1/4-inch-diced fresh mangoes
2 C. orange juice
2 tbsp extra-virgin olive oil
1 seedless cucumber, cut into 1/4-inch dice
1 small red bell pepper, seeded and cut into 1/4-inch dice
1 small onion, cut into 1/4-inch dice

2 medium garlic cloves, minced
1 small jalapeno pepper, seeded and minced
3 tbsp fresh lime juice
2 tbsp chopped fresh parsley
Salt and freshly ground black pepper

Directions

1. In a blender, add the mangoes, oil and orange juice and pulse till pureed.
2. Transfer the mango puree in a bowl with the remaining all ingredients and mix well.
3. Refrigerate till serving.

Cambodian
Gazpacho Soup

Prep Time: 40 mins
Total Time: 40 mins

Servings per Recipe: 4

Calories	467.3
Fat	29.6g
Cholesterol	0.0mg
Sodium	2927.3mg
Carbohydrates	52.8g
Protein	6.4g

Ingredients

1 small onion, chopped
1 tbsp salt
1 quart orange juice, squeezed
1 C. lime juice, squeezed
1 tbsp sugar
2 tsp salt
1/2 tsp black pepper

1 tsp garlic, chopped
2 tbsp extra virgin olive oil
3 avocados, cubed
2/3 C. button mushroom, sliced
2 C. plum tomatoes, diced without pulp
1 tbsp cilantro, chopped

Directions

1. In a colander, add the chopped onion and sprinkle with the salt generously.
2. Keep aside for about 25-30 minutes.
3. Now, rinse the onion under the cold running water to remove the salt completely.
4. Drain the onion well and then, squeeze the excess moisture.
5. In a bowl, add the garlic, oil, lime juice, orange juice, sugar, salt and black pepper and mix until well combined.
6. Add the mushroom, avocado, onion and tomatoes and mix until well combined.
7. Refrigerate for about 1 1/2 hours.
8. Stir in 1 tbsp of the chopped cilantro and enjoy.

FRUIT
Gazpacho

Prep Time: 10 mins
Total Time: 30 mins

Servings per Recipe: 6
Calories	110 kcal
Fat	4.8 g
Carbohydrates	16.4g
Protein	1.8 g
Cholesterol	0 mg
Sodium	3 mg

Ingredients

2 C. 1/4-inch-diced watermelon
2 C. orange juice
2 tbsp extra-virgin olive oil
1 seedless cucumber, cut into 1/4-inch dice
1 small yellow bell pepper, seeded and cut into 1/4-inch dice
1 small onion, cut into 1/4-inch dice

2 medium garlic cloves, minced
1 small jalapeno pepper, seeded and minced (optional)
3 tbsp fresh lime juice
2 tbsp chopped fresh parsley
Salt and freshly ground black pepper

Directions

1. In a blender, add 1/2 C. of the watermelon, orange juice and oil and pulse till smooth.
2. Transfer the mixture into a bowl with the remaining ingredients and stir to combine.
3. Refrigerate before serving.

Gazpacho
of Independence

Prep Time: 10 mins
Total Time: 15 mins

Servings per Recipe: 6
Calories	378.5
Fat	36.5g
Cholesterol	0.0mg
Sodium	619.8mg
Carbohydrates	12.7g
Protein	2.6g

Ingredients

2 lbs tomatoes, stems removed, cleaned
1 garlic clove, peeled
1/2 an onion, white, diced and peeled
1 green sweet pepper, rinsed, diced, seed removed
1 cucumber, about 6-7 inches long, peeled
1/4 tsp ground cumin

3 tbsps red wine vinegar
1/2 tbsp salt
1 C. virgin olive oil
1 piece French bread

Directions

1. Let your bread sit submerged in water for 5 mins then remove the liquids and squeeze the bread to drain more water from it.
2. Add the following to the bowl of a food processor: moist bread, tomatoes, cucumber, garlic, pepper, and onions.
3. Pulse the mix until everything is smooth and all the pieces are small, then add in the cumin, vinegar, salt, French bread (broken into pieces), and olive oil.
4. Pulse everything again until it is creamy.
5. Place everything in a bowl and put the mix in the fridge until it is chilled.
6. Enjoy.

SPICY
Summer-Time Gazpacho

Prep Time: 15 mins
Total Time: 25 mins

Servings per Recipe: 8
Calories   115.4
Fat   5.6g
Cholesterol   0.0mg
Sodium   536.8mg
Carbohydrates   15.5g
Protein   2.8g

Ingredients

3 tbsps extra virgin olive oil
3/4 C. chopped red onion
3/4 C. chopped red bell pepper
3/4 C. chopped green bell pepper
3 large garlic cloves, diced
2 C. organic tomato juice
2 C. spicy vegetable juice
1 C. Clamato juice
1 C. organic chicken broth
3 tbsps parsley

3 tbsps basil
3 tbsps chives
kosher sea salt & freshly ground black pepper
2 C. seeded diced fresh tomatoes
1 cucumbers, diced

Directions

1. Begin to stir fry your garlic, onion, and bell peppers for 10 mins.
2. Then combine in the chives, tomato juice, basil, v-8, chicken broth, and clamato.
3. Stir the mix then add in some black pepper and salt.
4. Get everything boiling then shut the heat and combine in the cucumber and tomatoes.
5. Stir the mix again then place the gazpacho in a bowl and place a covering of plastic on the bowl.
6. Put everything in the fridge for 8 hrs.
7. Now stir the gazpacho again and divide the mix between serving dishes.
8. Top each dish with croutons and cheese.
9. Enjoy.

Bright
Summertime Gazpacho

Prep Time: 20 mins
Total Time: 20 mins

Servings per Recipe: 6	
Calories	147 kcal
Fat	5 g
Cholesterol	26.2g
Sodium	1.6 g
Carbohydrates	0 mg
Protein	5 mg

Ingredients

2 C. 1/4-inch-diced fresh mangoes
2 C. orange juice
2 tbsp extra-virgin olive oil
1 seedless cucumber, cut into 1/4-inch dice
1 small red bell pepper, seeded and cut into 1/4-inch dice
1 small onion, cut into 1/4-inch dice
1 small jalapeno pepper, seeded and minced

3 tbsp fresh lime juice
2 medium garlic cloves, minced
2 tbsp chopped fresh parsley
Salt and freshly ground black pepper

Directions

1. In a blender, add the mangoes, oil and orange juice and pulse till pureed.
2. Transfer the mango puree in a bowl with the remaining all ingredients and mix well.
3. Refrigerate till serving.

ENJOY THE RECIPES?

KEEP ON COOKING
WITH 6 MORE FREE COOKBOOKS!

Visit our website and simply enter your email address to join the club and receive your 6 cookbooks.

http://booksumo.com/magnet

https://www.instagram.com/booksumopress/

https://www.facebook.com/booksumo/

Printed in Great Britain
by Amazon